# BISHOP
# DANIEL A. PAYNE
## GREAT BLACK LEADER

## RUDINE SIMS BISHOP

JUST US BOOKS

*Dedication*

*Honoring my first church home*
*Bethel AME Church, Pottsville, PA*

*Where Bishop Payne once stopped by and left a lasting impression*

Printed in Canada
12 11 10 9 8 7 6 5 4 3 2 1
Library of Congress Cataloging-in-Publication data is available.

ISBN: 978-1-933491-13-4
Credits for illustrations and photographs appear at the end of this book.

# CONTENTS

# FOREWORD

Rudine Sims Bishop has written a book that is not only appropriate for the time in which Daniel Payne lived, but also for the Obama era of which we are now all a part. Bishop Daniel Payne: Great Black Leader is a significant work because it captures the life of one of the world's most extraordinary human beings. Bishop Payne has often been defined by his role in founding America's first university owned and operated by African Americans. The impact of this singular event has spawned generations of young people who otherwise would not have had an opportunity to participate in higher learning.

Payne's tenacity was reflected not only in his focus on higher education in general, but also in the preparation of young men who occupied various pulpits. These were persons who often came off plantations, where they had been denied, by virtue of race, access to the White institutions that existed. As they were educated, it created a rift in the AME Church; bishops debated issues regarding the free form worship that slaves practiced and the literary form of worship of formally educated Blacks. The remnants of that battle are still evident as some members of the AME Church seek a quiet, low-toned worship experience while others prefer a more spirited, lively style of worship.

Payne truly believed that God had called him for the work of teaching and it was exemplified in his testimony. He proclaimed the Lord revealed to him: "I have set thee apart to educate thyself in order that thou mayest be an educator to thy people." By every definition Bishop Payne was not simply a teacher, but a very extraordinary one, taking the time to teach himself Greek, Latin, geography, map-making, English grammar, mathematics and science.

With so much focus today on what Barack Obama's election means, it is good to know that preceding him was Daniel Payne, on whose shoulders President Obama stands. Times have changed, but African Americans are still in need of knowledge about Daniel Payne, whose life is a textbook on excellence. The African Methodist Episcopal Church and Wilberforce University represent significant building blocks that allowed African Americans in the post-slave era to dare to dream. More than dreams, they were hallmarks of hope for people who could have easily given up. Change as we know it today may well have sprouted from the roots that were planted by Daniel Alexander Payne. I am proud to have had the opportunity to walk in his foot path by serving as the 18th President of Wilberforce University, which still stands as a center of hope, promise and possibility for this and future generations.

*—The Honorable Reverend Floyd H. Flake, D. Min.*
*Pastor, Greater Allen A.M.E. Cathedral of New York,*
*Retired U.S. Congressman*

# PREFACE

While doing research for a book on African-American children's literature, I learned that some of the earliest writing for children by African Americans can be found in church publications. The name of one church leader, Bishop Daniel Alexander Payne of the African Methodist Episcopal (AME) Church, kept turning up in discussions of these publications and of efforts to educate African Americans in the 1800s. As I discovered more information about Bishop Payne, I was captivated by the life story of this five-foot, 100-pound little giant who rose from an orphaned carpenter's apprentice, to a bishop, to president of the first African-American university and one of the most influential African-American leaders of the nineteenth century. He was a contemporary of Abraham Lincoln and Frederick Douglass, and he interacted with both of them as well as with numerous other well-known American and European leaders. Although his family was free, he was born in Charleston, South Carolina at a time when most African Americans were being held in slavery, and the laws of the land kept slavery and discrimination legal. When I read about his efforts to teach himself, his crusade for education for African Americans, his leadership roles, and his determination to hold to and share his religious faith—all in spite of the many obstacles placed in his path—I was convinced he was someone today's young people would like to know about. When I discovered that Bishop

BISHOP DANIEL A. PAYNE

Payne had once visited the little AME church in Pottsville, Pennsylvania where I grew up, I felt that I was the one who should tell his story.

This book would not have been possible, however, without the aid and support of several people. First I want to thank my publishers Cheryl and Wade Hudson for expressing interest in the book even before it was written and for helping to make it better than it was when they first saw the manuscript. Thanks to Miss Jacqueline Brown, archivist at the Wilberforce University Library, for making the library's archival materials on Bishop Payne accessible to me, and for securing copies of important images. I also thank Ohio State University colleagues Dr. Susan Fisher and Dr. Barbara Bloettschner, of the Department of Entomology, who provided information that allowed me to identify the caterpillar that, in Bishop Payne's view, led to some life-changing events. I am grateful to Dr. Ricardo Bessin, Dept. of Entomology at the University of Kentucky, who promptly and generously gave me permission to use, without a fee, his beautiful color photograph of a cecropia moth caterpillar. Dr. Pete Yasenchak, of the Schuylkill County Historical Society searched for a photograph of Bethel AME Church in Pottsville, PA and, in the absence of a suitable photograph in his files, asked his wife to go out and take some photographs, which they sent to me by e-mail on the very day that I called.  Thanks to him and to Mrs. Yasenchak. And finally, my eternal gratitude to my husband, one-man support team, and favorite photographer, Dr. James J. Bishop, who drove to Wilberforce and Payne Theological Seminary with me and took numerous photographs, including the one that forms the backdrop for a number of images in the book.

*–Rudine Sims Bishop*
*March 16, 2009*

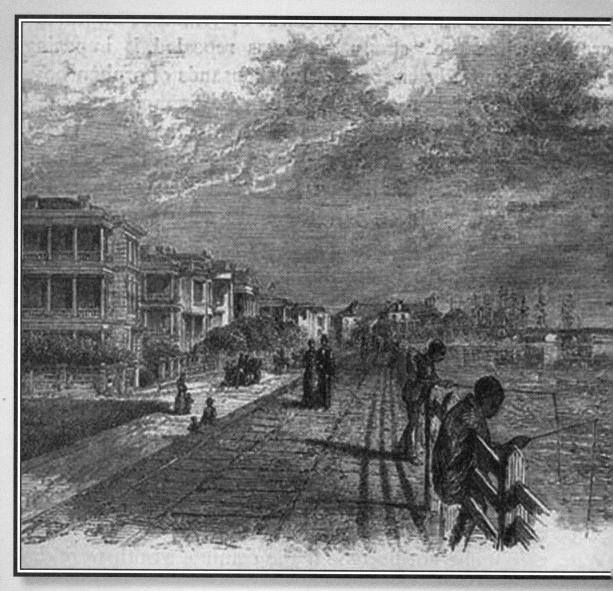

*The Battery in Charleston, South Carolina. During the early nineteenth century, Charleston was the cultural and economic center of the South. It was a busy seaport, a major center for the slave trade, and a summer resort for wealthy planters with big city homes.*

# CHARLESTON, SOUTH CAROLINA

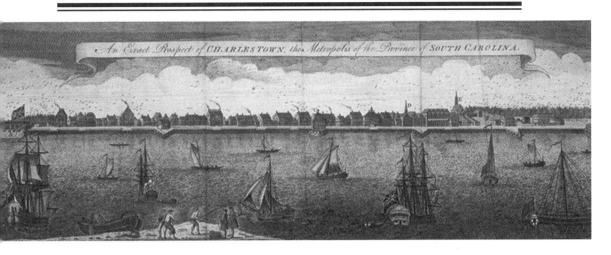

*"I was the child of many prayers."*
—Daniel A. Payne, *Recollections of Seventy Years*

**R**IDING HIGH on his father's shoulders, little Daniel Alexander Payne had a breathtaking view of the excitement. Lights were shining all over Charleston, South Carolina. The War of 1812 had ended and the city was celebrating the peace. Daniel was about four years old, and this special moment with his father was one of his earliest and happiest memories. It must have been a happy time for his father, too. London Payne, who was a man of faith and a leader in his church, believed that Daniel was the answer to his prayers. He had very much wanted a son, and he had promised that if his baby were a boy, he would dedicate the child to God and name him after the prophet Daniel from the Bible. Little Daniel was born on February 24,

1

1811, and soon after that, London Payne dedicated his son to God twice—once when Daniel was baptized in church, and again right after the ceremony, at their home on Swinton Lane in Charleston.

Charleston was a bustling center of trade and commerce, and home to thousands of Black people. In fact, Black people made up the majority of the city's population, even though most of them were being held in slavery. Charleston's prosperity depended on slave labor. Enslaved workers harvested the rice and cotton on nearby plantations, loaded and unloaded ships in the busy harbor, and helped to build new ships. Yet these all-important workers were considered property, like mules or farmland. They had no rights and few opportunities, and they were hungry for freedom and for knowledge that would help them make their lives better. Charleston was also home to many free persons of color—Black people who were not enslaved. Many of them were skilled workers who made a decent living, but they, too, were hungry for education. Some of them even set up schools for fellow Blacks, both free and enslaved.

London Payne and his family were legally free, and therefore

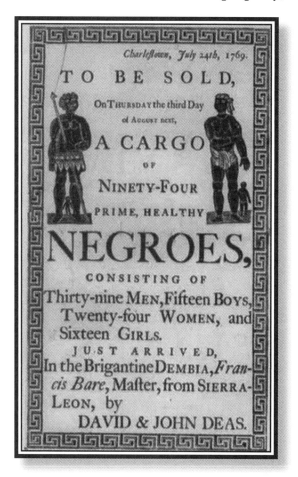

*A broadside advertising the sale of ninety-four newly arrived Africans in Charleston. They would become slaves.*

better off than many of their Black neighbors. But he knew what it was to be enslaved. He had been born free in Virginia, but when he was just a young boy, some sailors had kidnapped him, taken him to Charleston, and sold him as a slave to a man who painted signs and houses. When London was grown he had to pay a thousand dollars to buy the freedom that was already rightfully his. Because he knew the importance of education, he started teaching his son the alphabet and

*Silhouette of Martha Payne.*

some beginning reading when Daniel was only three or four. It was one of the last things London Payne was able to do for his son. He died when Daniel was about four and a half years old.

Daniel's mother, Martha Payne, was Catawba Indian and Black. She was a gentle woman with a pleasant personality and deep religious faith. After her husband died, Martha often took her little Daniel by the hand and led him to the Methodist church, where he sat beside her listening to the service. This lasted only about five years, for when Daniel was about nine and a half years old, Martha

ACCORDING TO THE UNITED STATES CENSUS BUREAU, IN 1810, THE YEAR BEFORE DANIEL PAYNE WAS BORN, THERE WERE 1,191,362 BLACK AMERICANS HELD IN SLAVERY. IN CHARLESTON THERE WERE 11,568 WHITES, 11,671 SLAVES AND 1,472 FREE PEOPLE OF COLOR. THE POPULATION OF FREE BLACK AMERICANS WAS 186,446.

Payne died of tuberculosis. But with their strong faith and their great respect for learning, Martha and London Payne had introduced Daniel to the two big passions of his life—religion and education.

With Martha's death Daniel had become an orphan, but he did have an older married sister and a great-aunt, Sarah Bordeaux. Aunt Sarah took him in and cared for him as if he were her own son. For two years Daniel attended a school established for poor and orphaned Black children by the Minor's Moralist Society, a group of free men of color. After that, he attended the most popular "colored" school in the city, run by Thomas Bonneau. Daniel was probably one of the smallest boys in his age group, but when it came to learning, he was a champion. He was almost always at the head of his class. By the time he was twelve, Daniel had learned about as much as Mr. Bonneau's school could teach him, and it was time to learn a trade. For four

IN 1822, WHEN DANIEL WAS ELEVEN YEARS OLD, DENMARK VESEY, A FREE BLACK CARPENTER AND A LEADER IN CHARLESTON'S AFRICAN METHODIST EPISCOPAL CHURCH, PLANNED A LARGE AND SOPHISTICATED SLAVE REVOLT. A NERVOUS SLAVE BETRAYED THE PLOT AND VESEY AND HIS FELLOW REBELS WERE HANGED BEFORE THEY COULD CARRY IT OUT. VESEY'S CHURCH WAS BURNED DOWN. HIS PASTOR WAS THE REV. MORRIS BROWN, WHO ESCAPED FROM CHARLESTON AND LATER BECAME THE SECOND BISHOP IN THE AME CHURCH THE 56 BULL STREET RESIDENCE IN CHARLESTON (ABOVE) IS BELIEVED T BE THE HOME OF DENMARK VESEY.

BISHOP DANIEL A. PAYNE

and a half years he was an apprentice to his sister's husband, James Holloway, who was a carpenter. For Daniel, the best thing about working with his brother-in-law was that while he was learning carpentry, he could also make time to read. One day he came across a book that "became the turning point" of his life. The author was the Rev. John Brown, a minister from Scotland, who wrote that he had taught himself to read Latin, Greek, and Hebrew. Daniel thought, "If Brown learned Latin, Greek, and Hebrew without a living teacher, why can't I?" He decided to try, and thanks to the Rev. Brown's example, Daniel became a lifelong autodidact, a person who teaches himself.

*Toussaint L'Ouverture, Haiti's revolutionary leader, was Daniel's childhood hero.*

He began by reading every book he could get his hands on. Like many young boys, he especially enjoyed the stories of men of action. He admired freedom fighters such as Robert the Bruce and William Wallace (Brave Heart), who had fought for Scotland's freedom from England. But his main hero was Toussaint L'Ouverture, a Black man who led the fight to free Black people in Haiti from slavery. Daniel thought he too would become a soldier and go fight with the Haitian people. But one night in a dream he became a fighting soldier, witnessing the terrible sights and hearing the awful sounds of battle. He was horrified; the dream showed him that he could never be a soldier at war.

When he was about seventeen, Daniel realized what he was meant to do instead. As his parents had taught him, he had made prayer a part of his daily life. Even when he was a child, he had prayed often, asking God to make him a good boy. One day he was in his room praying, when suddenly he felt as if hands were pressing down on his shoulders, and a voice deep inside was saying, "I have set thee apart to educate thyself in order that thou mayest be an educator to thy people." He believed it was the voice of God, calling him to teach.

Before he would start to teach others, though, Daniel worked even harder at educating himself. He spent all his spare money buying books, and all his spare time studying. He earned book money by making "tables, benches, clothes-horses, and corset-bones," which he sold in the public market on Saturday nights. During the week at mealtime, he would eat as quickly as he could and use the rest of the time to read. After work he would read until midnight. Then he would get up at four o'clock in the morning and read by candlelight. He not only read books, he also drew pictures and wrote poetry. He would read, write and draw for two hours, until six, when it was time to go to work in the carpenter shop. Daniel followed this self-made schedule as strictly as a soldier following orders. Even though he must have been exhausted some days, he kept to it until he felt ready to answer the call to teach.

# FREE PEOPLE OF COLOR

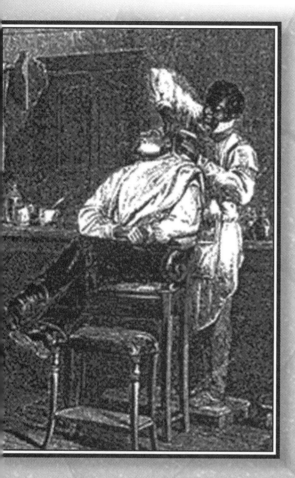

By the 1800s, thousands of free people of color were living in cities such as Charleston. Many made a living in trades such as barbering (left), carpentry, and tailoring. In 1838, a Philadelphia abolitionist group reported (below) that, in spite of discrimination, the city's free people of color owned property, paid taxes, and looked after each other's welfare.

*Charleston "Free Badge"*
*From 1783 to 1789 in Charleston all free persons of color fifteen and older were required to buy from the city and wear a copper badge like the one above. It shows a "liberty hat" on a pole.*

THE

PRESENT STATE AND CONDITION

OF THE

FREE PEOPLE OF COLOR,

OF THE

CITY OF PHILADELPHIA

AND

ADJOINING DISTRICTS, AS EXHIBITED BY THE

REPORT

OF A

COMMITTEE OF THE PENNSYLVANIA SOCIETY

FOR

PROMOTING THE ABOLITION OF SLAVERY, &c.

Read First Month (Jan.) 5th, 1838.

PHILADELPHIA:
PUBLISHED BY THE SOCIETY.
MERRIHEW AND GUNN, PRINTERS,
No. 7 Carter's Alley.
1838.

*Zion School for Colored Children, Charleston, 1866. After the Civil War, freed African Americans flocked to schools like this, established by the government and churches. Before then free people of color, especially in the South, had to provide their own schools.*

# A LIVING TEXTBOOK,
# AN EXTRAORDINARY TEACHER

*"Pursue knowledge wherever it is to be found. Like the air you breathe, it may be inhaled everywhere."*
advice from John Bachman as Daniel Payne was leaving Charleston.
—Daniel A. Payne, *Recollections of Seventy Years*

DANIEL WAS 18 when he opened his first school. It was only one room in the home of Caesar Wright, and there were only six students. During the day he taught Mr. Wright's three children, and at night he taught three enslaved adults. He charged 50¢ a month for each student, but $3.00 a month was not nearly enough to live on. After about a year of struggling to make ends meet, he closed the school and started searching for another way to make a living. He went to see a rich slaveholder who was looking to hire a free young Black man to go to the West Indies with him and help with his business. Trying to persuade Daniel to take the job, the slaveholder asked, "Daniel, do you know what makes the difference between master and servant?" Answering his own question, he continued, "Nothing but superior knowledge—nothing but one man knowing more than another. Now, if you will go with me, the knowledge you

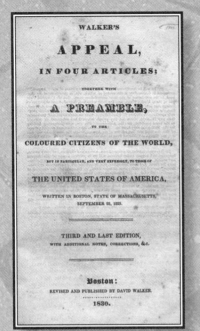

WALKER'S

**APPEAL,**

IN FOUR ARTICLES;

TOGETHER WITH

**A PREAMBLE,**

TO THE

COLOURED CITIZENS OF THE WORLD,

BUT IN PARTICULAR, AND VERY EXPRESSLY, TO THOSE OF

THE UNITED STATES OF AMERICA,

WRITTEN IN BOSTON, STATE OF MASSACHUSETTS,
SEPTEMBER 28, 1829.

THIRD AND LAST EDITION,

WITH ADDITIONAL NOTES, CORRECTIONS, &c.

Boston:

REVISED AND PUBLISHED BY DAVID WALKER.

1830.

THE SAME YEAR DANIEL OPENED HIS SCHOOL, 1829, DAVID WALKER, A FREE BLACK MAN LIVING IN BOSTON PUBLISHED HIS *APPEAL*, (LEFT). THIS PAMPHLET ATTACKED SLAVERY AND URGED SLAVES IN THE UNITED STATES OF AMERICA TO REVOLT. WALKER USED SAILORS TO SEND AND DISTRIBUTE COPIES OF HIS PAMPHLET IN THE SOUTHERN STATES. THIS ANGERED SLAVEHOLDERS AND THEIR SUPPORTERS. WALKER WAS FOUND DEAD AT HIS HOME IN 1830, BUT HIS *APPEAL* CONTINUED TO INSPIRE ENSLAVED AND FREE BLACKS TO AGITATE FOR THE ABOLITION OF SLAVERY FOR YEAR AFTER HIS DEATH.

ONE OF THE FIRST SCHOOLS TO EDUCATE BLACKS WAS THE NEW YORK AFRICAN FREE SCHOOL (RIGHT), ESTABLISHED IN 1787. THIS SKETCH WAS DRAWN BY PATRICK REASON, A 13-YEAR OLD STUDENT.

may acquire will be of more value to you than the money you will earn." Right then Daniel understood what people meant when they said, "knowledge is power." He was inspired—not to go with the slaveholder, but to go after more knowledge. He was determined to gain as much knowledge as the slaveholders had, and he intended to share his knowledge with as many Black people as he could reach.

Daniel re-opened his school, and this time it was a big success. He continued to teach himself—Greek and Latin, geography, map-making, English grammar, mathematics, and science. He was curious about everything, in one case perhaps too curious. On February 12, 1831 the sky over Charleston turned dark in the middle of the day. The moon passed between the earth and the sun, causing a total solar eclipse. Daniel could not resist studying this rare event.

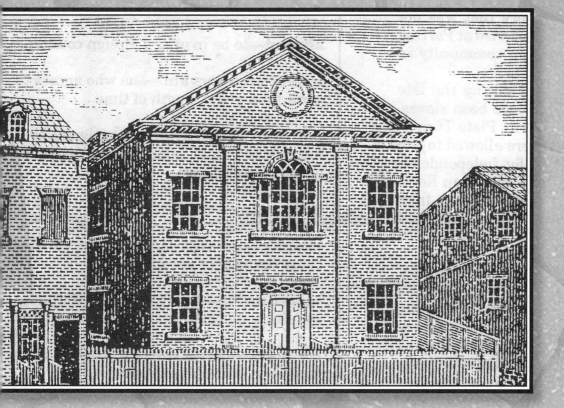

He watched the eclipse with his naked eye, which was a terrible mistake. During an eclipse the light from the sun is so concentrated that it can cause blindness by burning the retina in the back of the eye. It is like using a magnifying glass to burn a piece of paper by focusing the sun's rays on one spot. For three weeks after the eclipse, Daniel could not read at all; every time he opened a book the pages looked like black sheets. Eventually he was able to read again, but he never fully recovered his eyesight.

All his reading and studying probably made Daniel the best-educated "colored" teacher in Charleston. He may also have been the most enthusiastic. He loved teaching, and his students caught his excitement. His school soon became the most popular of the five "colored" schools in the city; it grew to about sixty students. Twice

*Dr. John Bachman, a Lutheran minister and naturalist, was a major influence on Daniel during his early years as a teacher. Dr. Bachman was well known for his collaboration with John James Audubon and wrote the text for Audubon's illustrations in the book,* The Quadrapeds of North America. *Dr. Bachman was the founder of Newberry College in South Carolina and a man of great stature and influence in the Luthern Church.*

he had to move to larger spaces, the last time to a school that had been built especially for him. He became so well known that two teachers from other schools in the city came to him to learn science. He willingly shared his knowledge.

Daniel's school was probably just one large room. There were few, if any textbooks, but Daniel himself was a living textbook, and he brought the natural world into his classroom. On Saturdays he and some of the boys in his class would go into the woods to search for plants and animals to bring back to the school. He taught his students how to draw flowers, fruit and animals on paper and on velvet cloth. He collected insects, toads, snakes, young alligators, fish and young sharks for his students to study. He cleaned and preserved the animals, then hung them on the classroom walls. Daniel even cooked and tasted the meat of the animals he captured— all except toads and snakes—so he could learn as much as possible about them. Outside was gym equipment that Daniel had made, and when the students needed a recess, he would lead them in sports and games. Daniel's teaching methods were far ahead of his time.

*Cecropia moth caterpillar, America's largest moth, was probably the type of worm Daniel received. He wrote that it was about the size of a man's middle finger, blue and gold, with black and gold horns running along its body and around its head. As a curious scientist, Daniel was determined to learn everything possible about this beautiful creature.*

A good deed and the gift of a caterpillar helped to change Daniel's life. Daniel let a fatherless boy attend his school free of charge. The boy's sister was grateful and, knowing of Daniel's interest in science, she sent to school an unusual caterpillar she had found. Daniel could not identify the caterpillar, so he asked Dr. John Bachman, a famous naturalist and Lutheran minister, to identify it and keep it in his studio. Dr. Bachman agreed and invited Daniel to visit from time to time to watch the caterpillar's progress. They had long conversations while they explored Dr. Bachman's garden and his insect collection. Dr. Bachman was very impressed with Daniel's knowledge and his intelligence. A few years later, a letter from Dr. Bachman, full of Daniel's praises, opened the way for Daniel to go to college. Near the end of his life Daniel wrote that the hand of God must have been in that lowly worm.

Daniel's school flourished for about four years. Then one summer day in 1834, he sent three of his students to a nearby plantation to collect a live snake, a highland moccasin that Daniel had paid a slave on the plantation to catch for him. But before they could collect the snake, the boys ran into the plantation owner, Mr. Kennedy, and his son. They asked many questions about the things students were learning at Daniel's school. The Kennedys, who were important men in the area, were impressed with the answers, but they were not pleased. A school like Daniel's was a threat to slavery. His students might even gain more knowledge than the slaveholders!

That December a new law was passed in South Carolina. It would punish anyone who taught enslaved Blacks or free persons of color, or who kept a school for them. White persons would be fined $100 and sent to prison for six months. Free persons of color would be fined $50 and given fifty lashes with a whip. Enslaved persons would receive fifty lashes. The new law would take effect on April 1, 1835. Daniel decided to close his school. He would not risk being whipped and he could not afford the fine. He was heartbroken. He felt as if "some wild beast had plunged [its] fangs into [his] heart, and was squeezing out [his] life-blood." He even began to doubt God, but his doubt didn't last long. Calming himself by writing poetry, he poured out his feelings in a very long and sad farewell poem.

Once again Daniel was guided by a dream. This time he saw himself lifted up to the North, flying along the southern edges of the Great Lakes, wearing the pink robe—similar to a graduation gown—he always wore when he was teaching. He interpreted this to mean that he should go to a northern city, where he could teach without the restrictions he met in Charleston. Before he made his final decision, he sought the advice of some men he respected, including Dr. Bachman. They all agreed that he should go north, and they gave him letters that would introduce him to friends of theirs in New York and Philadelphia, important men who could help Daniel find work and get settled.

# THE MOURNFUL LUTE, OR THE PRECEPTOR'S* FAREWELL

*(Last three verses)*

*Pupils, attend my last departing sounds;*
*Ye are my hopes, and ye my mental crowns,*
*My monuments of intellectual might,*
*My robes of honor and my armor bright.*
*Like Solomon, entreat the throne of God;*
*Light shall descend in lucid columns broad,*
*And all that man has learned or man can know*
*In streams prolific shall your minds o'erflow.*

*Hate sin; love God; religion be your prize;*
*Her laws obeyed will surely make you wise,*
*Secure you from the ruin of the vain,*
*And save your souls from everlasting pain.*
*O fare you well for whom my bosom glows*
*With ardent love, which Christ my Savior knows!*
*For you I wept, and now for you I pray.*

*Farewell! Farewell! ye children of my love;*
*May joys abundant flow ye from above!*
*May peace celestial crown your useful days,*
*To bliss transported, sing eternal lays;*
*For sacred wisdom give a golden world,*
*And when foul vice his charming folds unfurl,*
*O spurn the monster, though his crystal eyes*
*Be like bright sunbeams streaming from the skies!*
*And I! O wither shall your tutor fly?*
*Guide thou my feet, great Sovereign of the sky.*

*A useful life by sacred wisdom crowned,*
*Is all I ask, let weal or woe abound!!*

*Daniel Alexander Payne, 1835*

*Poem written in grief after he felt forced to close his first school in Charleston.*

*\* A preceptor is a teacher.*

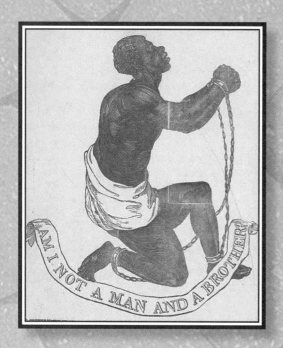

In July of 1835, a mob of citizens made a night time raid on the Charleston post office and ransacked the building (above). They tore open bundles of newspapers such as *The Liberator* and burned other abolitionist mail that they found. Note a sign reading "$20,000 Reward for Tappan" posted on the post office as bounty on the head of Arthur Tappan, founder and president of the American Anti-Slavery Society. The original caption read, "New method of assorting the mail, as practised by Southern slave-holders, or attack on the Post Office."

Am I not a Man and a Brother? (above left) was a popular image among abolitionists in England and the United States. Pro-slavery southerners hated and feared this kind of material.

On the last week of school, Daniel invited the parents of his pupils and people in the community to come and see what the children had been learning. Daniel was proud of all that they had accomplished. "But the last month, the last week, the last day, and the last hour of this interesting school had come, and it closed as it had begun—with singing and prayer—on the last day of March, 1835." Many people were sorry to see Daniel leave Charleston, and many of them helped him with things he would need for the journey. When it was time to leave, a large group of friends came to the dock to see him off and wish him well. On Saturday, May 9, 1835, amid many tears, Daniel Alexander Payne boarded a steamboat headed for New York City.

*Daniel A. Payne's signature.*

## THREE: 1835-1843
# FIRST YEARS IN THE NORTH

*"When God has a work to be executed he also chooses the man to execute it. He also qualifies the workman for the work . . . {t}he hour for the man and the man for the hour."*
—Daniel A. Payne, *Recollections of Seventy Years*

**SOON AFTER** Daniel arrived in New York on May 13, he took his letters of introduction and went to meet the people to whom they were addressed. On his final visit Daniel presented his letter from Dr. Bachman to the Rev. Daniel Strobel, a Lutheran minister. Rev. Strobel had just learned that some students at a college in Pennsylvania wanted to give money to educate a talented, religious young man of color, who could then help the free people of color in this country. After reading Dr. Bachman's letter, Rev. Strobel was certain that Daniel was exactly the young man the students were looking for, and that God must have sent him right at that moment. He urged Daniel to go and attend the school, the Lutheran Theological Seminary at Gettysburg. A seminary is a school that trains ministers, and Daniel protested that he wanted to be a teacher, not a preacher. Rev. Strobel convinced Daniel that a college education would make him a better teacher, and that he would not have to become

*Painting from life by A. Haffy. An inscription reads, "Rev. Daniel A. Payne, Minister of the African Methodist Episcopal Church."*

a minister. Daniel became the first Black student at the seminary.

While at Gettysburg, Daniel spent many hours reading and studying. He earned money to help with his expenses by doing odd jobs such as cutting wood, shining shoes, and shaving people's beards. He also stayed busy in the community. He started a Sunday School for "colored" children in the neighborhood, and recruited seminary students and townspeople as volunteer teachers. He organized a self-improvement group for "colored" women. He also held religious meetings. At one of those meetings, he spoke for three straight hours, and lost his voice for three weeks. Daniel refused to join the Methodist Episcopal Church in Gettysburg, because its leaders were in favor of slavery. Instead he attached himself to a small Black church in Carlisle, a nearby town. Daniel soon became an active church leader. He helped in the Sunday School and often spoke from the pulpit. Once he walked 25 miles from Gettysburg to Carlisle to take some textbooks to a class he had organized.

Although Daniel was often homesick for Charleston, he was happy with his studies, his church and community work. But one day while he was lying in bed reading, he felt a sharp pain in his left eye, as if a needle was being stuck into his eyeball. He had strained his optic nerve, and the doctor's only advice was to rest and wear tinted glasses. It took an entire year for Daniel's eye to heal, and since he could not read during that time, he could not keep up with his studies. He had to leave the seminary after only two years. Even though he had not finished his program, however, he was still qualified to become a minister.

Soon after he dropped out of the seminary, Daniel felt the call to preach. He was lying in bed one day, thinking about his future, when he sensed a pressure, which he thought was coming from God. He believed that God was calling him to "preach the gospel." Dan-

# WE ARE HERE AND ARE HERE TO STAY

WHEN DANIEL FIRST ARRIVED IN NEW YORK HE WAS URGED BY MANY OF THE PROMINENT WHITE MEN HE MET TO GO TO AFRICA RATHER THAN TO STAY IN THE UNITED STATES WHERE SLAVERY WAS STILL ENFORCED. DANIEL WAS OPPOSED TO THE IDEA, AND BEFORE HE WOULD ACCEPT A SCHOLARSHIP TO GETTYSBURG SEMINARY HE MADE SURE THAT THE LUTHERANS WHO WERE SPONSORING HIM WERE NOT PLANNING TO SEND HIM TO AFRICA AFTER HIS GRADUATION. THE SEMINARIANS AT GETTYSBURG WERE ABOLITIONISTS WHO WANTED TO HELP AFRICAN AMERICANS IN AMERICA. THE AMERICAN COLONIZATION SOCIETY (ACS) HAD BEEN FORMED IN 1817 IN ORDER TO SETTLE FREE BLACK AMERICANS IN AFRICA. MANY PROMINENT MEN BELONGED TO OR SUPPORTED THE GROUP, INCLUDING HENRY CLAY (MIDDLE LEFT), AND PRESIDENTS JAMES MADISON, JAMES MONROE AND THOMAS JEFFERSON. THE ACS RAISED MONEY BY SELLING LIFETIME MEMBERSHIPS IN THE SOCIETY FOR $30 EACH. MEMBERS RECEIVED A CERTIFICATE (BOTTOM LEFT) WITH A HENRY CLAY SIGNATURE. SOME BLACK LEADERS WERE ALSO IN FAVOR OF EMIGRATION BECAUSE THEY THOUGHT AFRICAN AMERICANS WOULD BE BETTER OFF IF THEY HAD THEIR OWN COUNTRY. FREDERICK DOUGLASS, HOWEVER, THE GREAT ABOLITIONIST AND ORATOR (TOP LEFT) WAS STRONGLY OPPOSED TO COLONIZATION AND SPOKE OUT AGAINST IT.

iel felt he had to answer the call. The Lutheran Church ordained him a minister, but they would not assign him to be the pastor of a Lutheran church. The president of the seminary, Dr. Schmucker, advised Daniel that he could be more helpful to people of color as a minister in a different denomination—the African Methodist Episcopal or AME (pronounced A-M-E) Church.

The AME Church had been organized many years earlier by Blacks protesting against discrimination in the Methodist Episcopal Church. Like other Black denominations, the AME Church was one of the few organizations that Black people controlled and operated, and it had thousands of members in the United States and in Canada. It was a network of individual churches located in many towns and cities; the church Daniel had attended in Carlisle was an AME church. Local AME churches served their people in many ways, not just by holding religious services. They ran schools, fed the hungry, took care of the sick, and taught people how to improve their daily lives. Many local AME churches also served as stations on the Underground Railroad, helping escaped slaves to freedom. This was exactly the kind of denomination Daniel was looking for.

When Daniel left Gettysburg, he headed for Philadelphia, intending to join the AME Church. Along the way, however, he met a friend of

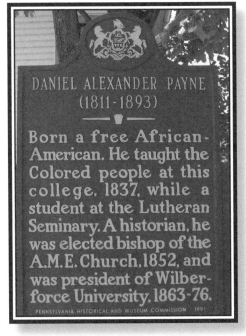

*A marker on the campus of Gettysburg College honoring Daniel Payne.*

*1906 photo of the AME church in Carlisle, PA, Daniel's church home when he was a student at Gettysburg Seminary.*

his father's who told him that people in the AME Church did not want educated ministers. According to his story, AME preachers often boasted that they had not "rubbed their heads against college walls," or studied Latin, Greek, or Hebrew. The church members would approve, answering "Amen!" or " Glory to God!" This report was only partly true, but Daniel believed it, and since he was an educated minister, he was afraid he would not be welcome in the AME Church. He accepted an invitation to become the pastor of a "colored" Presbyterian church in East Troy, New York.

Daniel was just twenty-six years old, young and inexperienced. He was very eager to save souls, and at a New Year's Eve service in 1837, he preached too long and too loud, trying to touch people's hearts. Then after the service he prayed aloud for the rest of the night. As a result, he lost his voice for a whole year and had to

*Bishop Morris Brown*

carry around a slate and chalk so he could write down what he wanted to say. On top of that, he caught a terrible cold, which kept him in bed for four months. Because he could no longer carry out his duties, he resigned as pastor of the church at East Troy. Still a teacher at heart, Daniel moved to Philadelphia, and in early 1840 opened a school on Spruce Street. He started with only three students, but by the end of the year, all the students from the city's two other private schools for people of color had transferred to his school. Three years later the school had 60 students.

In Philadelphia, Daniel came into contact with some of the leading members of the AME Church, including Bishop Morris Brown, the senior AME bishop, and J. J. G. Bias, a prominent Black doctor who was involved with the Underground Railroad. In fact, Daniel became a member of a group called the Vigilance Committee, which helped about 300 runaway slaves a year get to safety. Bishop Brown and Dr. Bias urged Daniel to join the AME Church, and the more he learned about it, the more he wanted to be a part of it. Daniel became a member of Bethel AME Church, known as Mother Bethel, and he soon became the very first seminary-trained AME minister.

In 1843 Bishop Brown appointed Daniel to be the pastor of Israel AME Church in Washington, D.C. This appointment presented two problems. First, Daniel did not want to leave his school in Philadelphia. Second, he had promised himself when he left Charleston that he would never again live in a place where slavery was legal. He had seen how cruel slavery was, and had felt its sting even though he was legally free. Once in Charleston, a White man had knocked Daniel down because he was carrying a cane. The man thought a cane was too fancy for a Black man. Daniel had fought back and had gone to jail briefly. In 1843 slavery was still legal in Washington, D. C. Free people of color had to get permission to live in the city, and pay a $1000 bond to guarantee "good behavior." Daniel thought this was insulting, but after praying about his decision, he chose to pay the money and go to Washington because he thought it was his Christian duty.

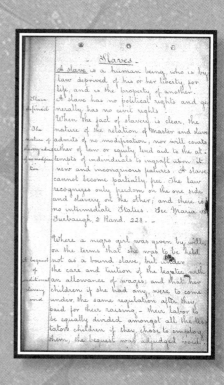

EVERY SLAVE STATE HAD SLAVE CODES LIKE THIS ONE FROM WASHINGTON, D.C. (RIGHT), DEFINING SLAVES AS PROPERTY. ABOLITIONIST SOJOURNER TRUTH (ABOVE) DEMANDED HUMANS RIGHTS FOR BLACK PEOPLE. HER LAWSUIT LED TO THE DESEGREGATION OF STREETCARS IN WASHINGTON, D.C.

# "WE WISH TO PLEAD OUR OWN CAUSE"

WHEN DANIEL ARRIVED IN NEW YORK HE WAS IMMEDIATELY INTRODUCED TO SOME OF THE LEADING FREE BLACK CITIZENS AND ANTISLAVERY ACTIVISTS IN THE CITY. AMONG THOSE HE MET WERE THE REV. PETER WILLIAMS, JR. WHO WAS THE FIRST AFRICAN-AMERICAN ORDAINED EPISCOPAL PRIEST, AND LEWIS TAPPAN, CO-FOUNDER OF THE ANTISLAVERY SOCIETY. HE ALSO MET CHARLES B. RAY, EDITOR OF *THE COLORED AMERICAN* NEWSPAPER; CHARLES REASON, THE FIRST AFRICAN-AMERICAN PROFESSOR AT A WHITE COLLEGE AND PRINCIPAL OF ONE OF THE COUNTRY'S BEST AFRICAN-AMERICAN SCHOOLS, AND ALEXANDER CRUMMEL, WHO WOULD BECOME A FAMOUS EPISCOPAL PRIEST, AN EDUCATOR, AND A MISSIONARY TO LIBERIA. THESE MEN WERE HIGHLY RESPECTED FOR SPEAKING OUT AGAINST SLAVERY AND ON BEHALF OF THE RIGHTS OF AFRICAN AMERICANS. SOME OF THEM HAD AN IMPORTANT INFLUENCE ON DANIEL'S THINKING. MOREOVER, THEY CONNECTED HIM TO A COMMUNITY OF ACTIVISTS WHOSE IMPACT WAS FELT NATIONALLY AND BEYOND.

*Rev. Peter Williams, Jr.*

*Lewis Tappan*

*Rev. Charles B. Ray*

*Charles L. Reason*

*Alexander Crummell*

*Rev. Samuel Cornish*

*John Brown Russwurm*

ALSO AMONG THE NEW YORKERS DANIEL MET WERE THE
REV. SAMUEL CORNISH AND JOHN BROWN RUSSWURM,
CO-EDITORS OF *FREEDOM'S JOURNAL* (BELOW), THE
FIRST NEWSPAPER OWNED AND OPERATED BY AFRICAN
AMERICANS. MANY OF THESE LEADERS WOULD PROBABLY
HAVE BEEN INVOLVED IN BLACK CONVENTIONS LIKE THE ONE
IN WASHINGTON, D.C. (ABOVE), WHERE DELEGATES SOUGHT
WAYS TO HELP THE PEOPLE IN THEIR COMMUNITIES.

# THE RISE TO LEADERSHIP

*"He was a child of the church, and in time became its father."*
—Frederick Douglass, Remarks on Bishop Daniel A. Payne
The Frederick Douglass Papers at the Library of Congress

WHEN DANIEL arrived at Israel AME Church he found a huge building with no seats on the lower level. He set to work with some carpenter's tools, and in a few weeks he had "fully seated" the church. That done, he turned his attention to the people. He set up a scientific and literary class in the church, and started the nation's first organization of Black pastors. He also launched a campaign to require that AME ministers had to be educated.

Very few AME ministers at the time had had an opportunity to get an advanced education. Some had very little education at all. Daniel was wise enough to know that if the AME Church was to continue to thrive and grow, its ministers needed to be educated. They needed to be able to understand and carry out the laws of the Church, manage Church affairs, interpret the Bible clearly, and teach their members how to live as good Christians. He also knew

that, unless ministers were educated, they would not be able to keep up with younger church members, who would have greater educational opportunities than their elders had.

As Daniel had heard, many AME ministers at the time were content to be uneducated. They and some of their members believed that all they needed was to be inspired or called by God; they thought education might even make them feel farther away from God. Others agreed with Daniel, including Bishop Morris Brown, who had very little schooling himself, but was highly respected for his wisdom and his leadership. Ministers and church members lined up on both sides of the issue; change would not come without a fight.

Daniel's main weapon in this battle was his pen. He wrote five long letters, or epistles, which he published in the AME Church magazine. His letters urged AME ministers to take every opportunity to educate themselves. He also argued that anyone who wanted to be an AME minister should be required to study certain subjects, including English grammar, arithmetic, geography, history, and theology or religious studies. A tide of angry letters arrived at the magazine, accusing Daniel of insulting AME ministers and doing the devil's work. Only a few took Daniel's side.

If Daniel was to win this battle, Church officials would have to vote in favor of his idea at an AME General Conference, a meeting held every four years. A General Conference was to be held in Pittsburgh in 1844, but Daniel was so upset about the ugly things his enemies had said and written that he decided not to attend. Bishop Brown persuaded him to change his mind. Daniel went to the conference and presented his resolution—to require ministers to study certain subjects—but he did not explain why it was a good idea because he thought most of the church leaders at the conference already agreed with him. He was wrong; the resolution was over-whelmingly defeated. There was such uproar over the vote that Daniel must have felt as if he had been thrown into a lion's den, like his namesake in the Bible, the prophet Daniel.

Just as an angel kept the lions from eating the prophet, Rev. Abram Lewis kept the delegates from defeating Daniel's resolution. The next morning, Rev. Lewis asked the delegates to reconsider. He then made a passionate speech in favor of the resolution. He argued that as leaders, the delegates had a duty to pave the way for the next generation. Rev. Lewis' speech was so convincing that even before he could finish, the delegates started shouting, "Give us the resolution! Give us the resolution." Then every delegate voted "yes" and Daniel's resolution became a part of the Discipline—the rules—of the AME Church. From then on, anyone who wanted to be an AME minister had to study the subjects Daniel had outlined in his letters. After the conference, he published eight more essays explaining and defending the new rules.

*First released in 1817,* The Doctrines and Discipline of the AME Church *is one of the first books published by African Americans. It is updated every four years.*

# "THIS FAR BY FAITH"

*Top left: Family worship on a South Carolina plantation. Top right: Pew and pulpit in a slave cabin. Center: An 1804 engraving of Mother Bethel AME Church, Philadelphia. This structure replaced the renovated blacksmith shop that was dedicated in 1794 and served as the congregation's first place of worship. Lower left: Baptist Church in Savannah, GA, founded in 1788. One of the first independent Black churches. Lower right: Richard Allen, founder and first bishop of the African Methodist Episcopal Church.*

*Top: Hymn from the current AME Hymnal, with words by Daniel A. Payne, showing his idea of proper worship. Bottom: Ring shout, Simons Island, GA. Worshippers danced, clapped and sang to convert sinners. Payne called the rings heathenish and disgraceful.*

MANY AFRICAN AMERICANS BECAME CHRISTIANS EARLY IN AMERICAN HISTORY. IN THE PLANTATION SOUTH, SLAVEHOLDERS TRIED TO CONTROL AFRICAN-AMERICAN WORSHIP AND THE BIBLE LESSONS SLAVES RECEIVED. SLAVEHOLDERS HELD AND ATTENDED WORSHIP SERVICES SET UP ON THEIR PLANTATIONS FOR THEIR FAMILIES AND THEIR SLAVES. ENSLAVED AFRICAN AMERICANS, HOWEVER, OFTEN WORSHIPPED ON THEIR OWN IN SECRET. EVENTUALLY, AFRICAN AMERICANS IN THE NORTH AND SOUTH BEGAN TO BREAK AWAY FROM WHITE-CONTROLLED CHURCHES, WHERE THEY OFTEN MET DISCRIMINATION. ONE OF THE FIRST BLACK BAPTIST CHURCHES WAS FORMED IN SAVANNAH, GEORGIA IN 1788. IN 1787, RICHARD ALLEN, A PHILADELPHIA METHODIST MINISTER AND FORMER SLAVE, LED A GROUP OF BLACK WORSHIPPERS TO FORM WHAT BECAME THE AFRICAN METHODIST EPISCOPAL CHURCH. AFRICAN-AMERICAN CHURCHES DEVELOPED VARIOUS FORMS OF WORSHIP, SOME OF WHICH, LIKE THE RING SHOUTS, RETAINED THE SPIRIT OF AFRICAN EXPRESSIONS. OTHERS STAYED CLOSE TO THE WORSHIP TRADITIONS AND ORGANIZATIONAL STRUCTURES OF THE PROTESTANT CHURCHES FROM WHICH THEY HAD BROKEN AWAY.

At the same General Conference, Daniel also introduced a number of other resolutions that changed or established new policies for the AME Church, or improved its organization. The only person who was more active than Daniel at that conference was Bishop Brown, who was in charge. Later, Daniel would write that the 1844 General Conference was the start of a new chapter in the history of the AME Church. It also marked a new chapter in his own life. He was only 33 years old. He had been in the AME Church just three years; yet he had become one of its best-known and most influential leaders.

In 1845 Daniel was assigned to Bethel AME Church in Baltimore, Maryland. There he opened the last elementary school he would operate himself. Like the others, the school was highly successful; within one year his school grew from three students to 50. While he was pastor at Bethel Baltimore, he also oversaw the building of a magnificent new church building. To raise money for the new building, Daniel presented a concert of sacred music. He hired James Fleet, the best Black musician in Washington, D.C., to put together a group of singers and musicians who played the flute, the guitar, the piano, and a large stringed instrument called the bass viol. Daniel wanted to be certain that all of the words, or lyrics, of the songs would be appropriate for church, so he wrote all the lyrics himself, and had them set to music. The concert was so successful that Daniel arranged for a second concert, featuring seven violins and a singer.

These were the first times that instrumental music had been played in an AME church. Thanks to Daniel's leadership, before long every AME Church wanted musical instruments. A few years earlier, Daniel had helped to introduce choir singing into the AME Church. When a few talented singers had formed a choir at Mother

Bethel in Philadelphia, some members were so unhappy they left the church for good. They had been used to everybody singing together, with one person leading. They thought a choir was the work of the devil. Daniel preached a special sermon that helped the people understand why sacred choir music was suitable for church services. They began to accept choir singing, and choirs soon became a normal part of AME churches.

Daniel also tried to change or do away with some forms of worship that he thought were not proper. He was especially unhappy about "Praying and Singing Bands," in which people would form a circle and clap their hands, stamp their feet and sing loudly. Usually these

*Bethel AME Church, Philadelphia, in 1973. "Mother Bethel," the first AME church. The fourth building on this site, it was dedicated by Daniel Payne in 1890.*

circles or rings would form after a church service, and last until late at night. It was the way the people expressed their religious spirit. He called the rings ridiculous and disgusting, especially because some of their songs were not the kind he thought appropriate for church. He called them "cornfield ditties," and gave an example in his journal:

> *Ashes to ashes, dust to dust*
> *If God won't have us, the devil must.*

This way of worshipping was very popular in many AME churches, and it took some courage to try to stop it. Daniel seldom lacked courage when he thought he was doing the right thing. He thought the Bible called for worship that was more quiet and reserved, so he discouraged the rings, and tried to stop them whenever he could. This battle went on for years, not just in Baltimore, but in many AME churches.

In 1847, when he was 36, Daniel married Mrs. Julia Farris, a widow from Washington, D.C. Less than a year later she gave birth to their daughter, who was named Julia Ann after her mother. Sadly, Daniel's wife died just a few hours after the baby was born. Daniel was heartbroken. He poured out his grief in a long poem, which he called "My Julia." But even more heartbreak was to come. Baby Julia Ann died when she was just nine months old. Once again Daniel turned to poetry to express his deep sadness. He took some comfort in his belief that his wife and daughter were with God.

While he was grieving the loss of his wife and baby, he also had to struggle with a small group of officers who tried to take over running Bethel Church. They did not succeed, but the conflict caused Daniel much distress. In 1848 he had been chosen to write the history of the AME Church, and early in 1850, he decided it was time to start working on that project. Daniel asked Bishop William Paul Quinn not to assign him to a church so he could work full time on the history project. The bishop refused this request, but he did assign Daniel to little Ebenezer AME Church in Baltimore, thinking that a smaller church would leave Daniel some time to work on the history.

When Daniel arrived at Ebenezer, however, he was met by a group of church officers who told him that the people of that church did not want him as their pastor. They said they knew he was a good person, but they thought he was too proud, he had too fine a carpet on his floor, he wouldn't have tea with the members, and he wouldn't let them sing their spiritual songs. Their charges were untrue (except the one about the songs) and Daniel thought they were unfair. He said to the officers, "Goodbye, brothers, I shall never cross your threshold again as your pastor." In a way, he was relieved, because he was now free to gather the information he needed to write the history of the AME Church.

For the next two years, 1850 to 1852, Daniel traveled to every AME church he could reach. He visited churches from Maryland to Maine, from New Jersey to Missouri, and as far south as New Orleans. He also visited all the AME churches in Canada. He collected all the written records he could find from each church—minutes of church meetings, pamphlets, programs, even scraps of paper people had written on. He read the journals of early AME Church leaders,

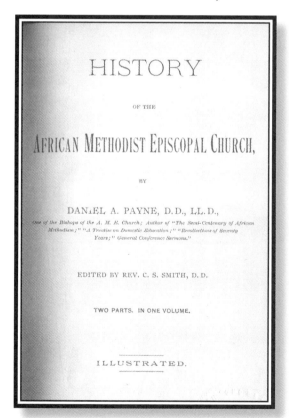

*Title page of Daniel Payne's* History of the African Methodist Episcopal Church, *published in 1891.*

# WHO IS SUFFICIENT?

Although Daniel Payne was not certain he was prepared for the position, he became one of the AME Church's most highly acclaimed bishops. This stained glass window honoring his legacy is in the chapel at Payne Theological Seminary. It shows a Bible in his hand and the original building of Wilberforce University above his head. At the bottom is the official motto of the AME Church, "God Our Father, Christ Our Redeemer, Man Our Brother."

*The Episcopal (bishop's) Seal of the AME Church, with the Church motto, was created under the supervision of Daniel A. Payne.*

especially the "father" and first Bishop of the AME Church, Richard Allen. He interviewed people who had known Richard Allen or who had participated in early AME Church meetings. Without Daniel's efforts, much of the early history of the AME Church might have been lost. Daniel had taught himself how to be a historian, but he did the job so well that even today anyone who wants to know the early history of the AME Church must read Daniel's book.

Daniel's last stop in his travels was New York City, to attend the 1852 AME General Conference. He had traveled so much he had nearly worn out his clothes; he even called himself the "shabbiest member of the conference." Nevertheless, Bishop Quinn ordered Daniel to deliver the opening sermon. Daniel had just two hours to prepare, but he delivered what some people think was his very best sermon. It was based on the Bible verse, "Who Is Sufficient for These Things?" (*II Corinthians, 2:16*). He preached about the duties of a minister, and about the qualities and characteristics a minister should have. His main point was that in all things a minister must model himself after Jesus Christ.

The most important business at the conference was to elect two new bishops. Daniel was one of four candidates. When the election results were announced and Daniel learned that he was to be a bishop, he "trembled from head to foot and wept." He was afraid he didn't have the physical strength, or the necessary knowledge to be a bishop. Furthermore even though he had tried all his life to model himself after Jesus, just as he had urged others to do in his sermon, he thought he still wasn't righteous enough for such a "high, holy, and responsible position." Nevertheless, on May 13, 1852, Daniel Alexander Payne was consecrated the sixth bishop of the African Methodist Episcopal Church, the highest office in the Church.

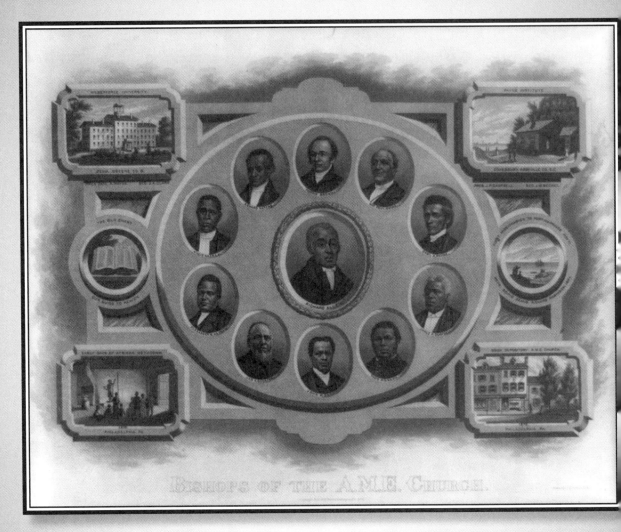

*The first eleven bishops of the AME Church, with the founder, Bishop Richard Allen, in the center. Daniel A. Payne is positioned at about 2 o'clock. These pioneers were very influential in the growth of the AME Church. The side images depict some important Church history and activities, including its book depository, two Church schools, and its first missionaries to Haiti.*

# A BATTLING BISHOP

*"His firmness of character was his fortress
and his good conscience his defense."*
—Benjamin F. Lee, *The AME Review,* July 1911

THE WORD "bishop" means "overseer" or "superinten-
dent," and for the next 41 years, Bishop Daniel Payne was one
of the most important overseers of the AME Church. Daniel was
a mite of a man, not more than five feet tall, thin and bony, and
he never in his life weighed more than 100 pounds, but he was a
mighty warrior for the AME Church and for Black people. One of
his main battles was for education. He believed the AME Church
needed not only educated ministers, but also educated members.
Wherever he went he either started or encouraged schools, Sunday Schools, study groups for ministers, and improvement societies for women. He also published poems, essays, and articles that
he thought would encourage Church members and others. He
thought Black people should be knowledgeable about many subjects, and he led the AME Church to publish a literary magazine,

which he edited for a while, and which lasted about seven years.

Soon after he was elected bishop, Daniel set out to oversee the churches in his district. He usually stayed in the homes of church members because in his day most hotels would not welcome Black guests. Most church members considered it an honor to have a bishop as a guest in their home, but Daniel often would not tell people who he was. He did not want to receive special treatment just because he was a bishop. Once, in a small town in Pennsylvania, a couple wouldn't let him into their house, only to discover when they went to church the next day that they had turned away the bishop. That day he preached a sermon about Christians' duty to be kind to one another, to be welcoming even to strangers, and not to judge people by their appearance. The couple was so embarrassed that even Daniel felt sorry for them. But he never hesitated to let people know when he thought they were not following the teachings of the Bible.

Daniel tried his best to live by his religious beliefs, and he expected other people to do the same. He thought that drinking alcohol and smoking tobacco were sinful, and he established or actively encouraged Temperance Societies, or anti-alcohol groups, among church members. One story says that at a conference banquet Daniel swept

*Page from the history of Bethel AME Church, Pottsville, PA, describing Payne's visit.*

BISHOP DANIEL A. PAYNE

all the bottles of wine off the long dinner table and threw them out the door as far as he could. Rules were important too. Another story says that when a distinguished visitor put his hat on a chair in Daniel's home, Daniel sat on the hat, and when it was time to leave, he gave the visitor back his crumpled hat, along with money for a new one. Daniel believed that hats should be placed on hat racks, not chairs.

Many of his battles were church battles. Soon after he became bishop, a White woman became a member of Mother Bethel. Many of the women members did not want her in their church, even though she was running a school for Black children. No doubt the women of Mother Bethel had been treated badly by White people who believed Black people were inferior. They were probably afraid this woman would look down on them, too. They demanded that the pastor expel her from the church, and he reluctantly carried out their wishes. At the next annual conference, Daniel refused to appoint the pastor to a church, saying, "The pastor who would turn away from God's sanctuary any human being on account of color was not fit to have charge of a gang of dogs." The pastor went to see Daniel, and angrily shook his fist in Daniel's face saying, "You dare to leave me without an appointment because of that White woman! Open your mouth, if you dare, and I will lay you flat upon the floor." Daniel simply remained calm and quiet, and after a few minutes, the pastor turned around and left. Another bishop, with Daniel's permission, assigned him to a church in Canada.

More often, Daniel had to fight prejudice and discrimination against himself. For the first two-thirds of his life, slavery was legal in the United States, and Black people all over the country were often deprived of their rights. On several occasions, Daniel was mistreated on trains or ships because he was Black, even though he paid as much for his ticket as everybody else. He was also not free to travel everywhere in the country. In 1856, he had to go to St. Louis, Missouri on church business. Missouri was a slave state, and it was against the law for him to come into the state to preach. Daniel was arrested, but a lawyer was able to get him released because officials had put the wrong name, Thomas Payne, on the legal papers. The lawyer warned Daniel's friend, Rev. Jordan Early, to whisk Daniel out of town before the officials could correct their mistake. Just as they were leaving in Jordan Early's carriage, an official arrived waving legal papers and shouting, "Stop that horse! Stop that horse!" But Rev. Early sped away and didn't stop until they were across the Mississippi River and in free territory in Illinois. In time the case was dismissed.

On April 14, 1862, Daniel took his fight against slavery directly to the President of the United States. On that day he went to the White House to talk to President Abraham Lincoln. Congress had voted to abolish slavery in Washington, D.C., and Daniel wanted to urge the President to sign the bill into law. It must have been a sight—the short, slightly built bishop, shaking hands with the very tall and lanky President. Congressman Washburn and General Shurz were also in the room at the time. Daniel spoke right up. He said to Lincoln, "I am here to learn whether or not you intend to sign the bill of emancipation." The President did not give a direct answer. He noted that some people had come that day to ask him not to sign. The general spoke in favor of the bill. Daniel told Lincoln that the "colored" people had been praying for him, as the President had asked the nation to do. Lincoln seemed pleased to hear that news, but he still would not give a yes or no answer. After

# THE SLOW DEATH OF SLAVERY

LEGAL SLAVERY DIED A VERY SLOW DEATH. IN 1846 DRED SCOTT, (ABOVE) A MISSOURI SLAVE WHO HAD LIVED IN FREE TERRITORY, SUED FOR HIS FREEDOM. IN 1857 THE SUPREME COURT RULED AGAINST HIM, SAYING THAT BLACK PEOPLE COULD NOT BE CITIZENS. FIVE YEARS LATER, EVEN AS ABRAHAM LINCOLN PREPARED TO FREE SLAVES IN REBEL STATES, HE STATED IN A LETTER TO EDITOR HORACE GREELEY (RIGHT) THAT HIS ACTUAL GOAL WAS TO SAVE THE UNION.

*President Abraham Lincoln*

## THE UNION AND SLAVERY.

### Letter From the President to Horace Greeley

EXECUTIVE MANSION,
WASHINGTON, Aug. 22, 1862.

*Hon. Horace Greeley:*

DEAR SIR: I have just read yours of the 19th, addressed to myself through the New-York Tribune. If there be in it any statements or assumptions of fact which I may know to be erroneous, I do not now and here controvert them. If there be in it any inferences which I may believe to be falsely drawn, I do not now and here argue against them. If there be perceptible in it an impatient and dictatorial tone, I waive it in deference to an old friend, whose heart I have always supposed to be right.

As to the policy I "seem to be pursuing," as you say, I have not meant to leave any one in doubt.

I would save the Union. I would save it the shortest way under the Constitution. The sooner the national authority can be restored the nearer the Union will be "the Union as it was." If there be those who would not save the Union unless they could at the same time *save* Slavery, I do not agree with them. If there be those who would not save the Union unless they could at the same time *destroy* Slavery, I do not agree with them. My paramount object in this struggle *is* to save the Union, and is *not* either to save or destroy Slavery. If I could save the Union without freeing *any* slave, I would do it, and if I could save it by freeing *all* the slaves, I would do it, and if I could save it by freeing *some* and leaving others alone, I would also do that. What I do about Slavery and the colored race, I do because I believe it helps to save this Union, and what I forbear, I forbear because I do *not* believe it would help to save the Union. I shall do *less* whenever I shall believe what I am doing hurts the cause, and I shall do *more* whenever I shall believe doing more will help the cause. I shall try to correct errors when shown to be errors; and I shall adopt new views so fast as they shall appear to be true views. I have here stated my purpose according to my view of *official* duty; and I intend no modification of my oft-expressed *personal* wish that all men, everywhere, could be free. Yours,

A. LINCOLN.

about 45 minutes, Daniel thought he should leave. He gave the President an AME newspaper and magazine so he could read about the progress of the AME Church. Two days later, on April 16, 1862, Abraham Lincoln signed the bill, and slavery was finally outlawed in the nation's capital.

By that time Daniel was living in Ohio. In the summer of 1854, he married Mrs. Eliza Clark, a widow with four children. Three were at home—Laura, who was eighteen; John, who was sixteen; and Augusta, who was six. Eliza also had an older stepson, Peter Clark. They lived in Cincinnati for a while, but Daniel thought the city was a terrible place to raise children; it was full of "corrupting influences." He searched for a place where the two younger children could go to school, and settled on a location near Xenia, Ohio, named Tawawa Springs, now called Wilberforce. It was on the grounds of what had once been a fancy resort hotel, with a large main building and several cottages. In July 1856, Daniel and his family happily moved into one of the smaller homes, which they named Evergreen Cottage. For the Payne family, the thick green grass and many trees were a welcome change; even their pet dog enjoyed the new surroundings. Evergreen Cottage would become Daniel's permanent home. Not surprisingly, one of the first things Daniel did was to organize a church in his home. He named it Zion's Chapel, and at first there were just four members. Later it was moved out of the cottage and became the Holy Trinity AME Church, which still exists.

The Cincinnati Conference of the Methodist Episcopal Church had bought the hotel and its grounds to use as a school for the education of "colored" people. The Methodists called the school a university, even though at the time it was more like an elementary and high school. They named the school after William Wilber-

*The original buildings of Wilberforce University, c. 1856.*

force, a famous British abolitionist who had fought fiercely against slavery in his country. Wilberforce University opened in October 1856, with M. M. P. Gaddis as its principal. There was also a Board of Trustees, a group of men who were responsible for watching over the school and managing its affairs. Four of the 24 Board members were "men of color." Daniel was the most active of the four. He lived on campus, he was a member of the Executive Committee, and in the summer, he was in charge of the school.

Most of the first students at Wilber-

*Daniel A. Payne and his second wife Eliza Clark Payne, c. 1854.*

force were from the South, the sons and daughters of slaveholding planters and enslaved women. There were no colleges and very few schools of any kind that those children could attend in the South, so their fathers sent them to Ohio to be educated. Then in 1861, the Civil War broke out, and most of the Southern slaveholders took their children out of school. With too few students and too little money, Wilberforce could not continue to operate. The Methodist Church closed the school in 1862. Early the next year, the university President, Dr. Richard Rust, informed Daniel that if the AME Church wanted to buy Wilberforce, they could have it for $10,000, which was the amount the Methodists still owed.

On March 10, 1863, Daniel was called to Cincinnati for a special meeting of the Wilberforce trustees. The State of Ohio wanted to buy the property, and they were willing to pay much more than $10,000. The trustees urged Daniel to buy the school for the AME Church. Daniel had sought advice from AME Church leaders, but he did not yet have permission to buy the school. Daniel said he needed three more months. The trustees said, "Now or never." It was after 9 p.m.; the state needed an answer by 11 o'clock the next morning. Daniel did not have even ten dollars in his pocket, let alone ten thousand dollars. But he stepped out on faith and declared, "In the name of the Lord I buy the property of Wilberforce for the African Methodist Episcopal Church."

By June, Daniel and his supporters had raised $2500 dollars for the first payment, and on June 11, 1863, the school was officially turned over to Daniel Alexander Payne, James A. Shorter and John G. Mitchell, as agents for the AME Church. With that, Wilberforce University became the first college in the United States owned and operated by Blacks. Daniel was elected president, making him the first Black president of an African-American college.

# THE CIVIL WAR

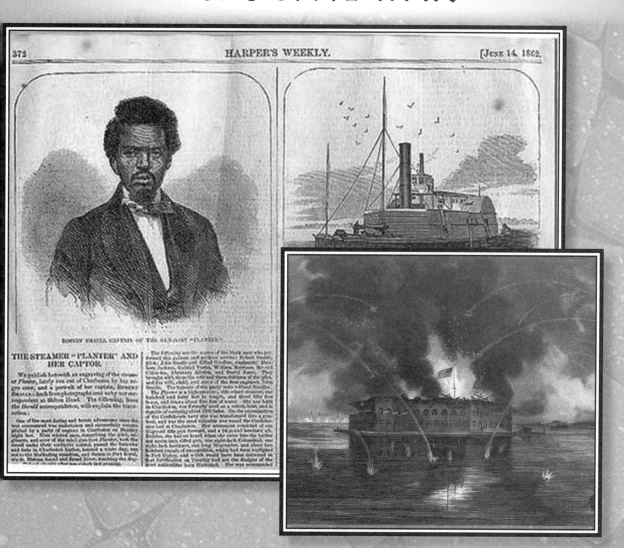

WHEN ABRAHAM LINCOLN WAS ELECTED PRESIDENT IN 1860, DANIEL'S HOME STATE, SOUTH CAROLINA, WAS THE FIRST TO SECEDE FROM THE UNITED STATES. SOUTH CAROLINA AND OTHER SOUTHERN STATES FORMED A REBEL CONFEDERATE GOVERNMENT AND ON APRIL 12, 1861, REBELS STARTED THE CIVIL WAR BY FIRING ON FORT SUMTER IN CHARLESTON HARBOR. IN MAY 1862 ROBERT SMALLS, (ABOVE LEFT) AN ENSLAVED SHIP'S PILOT, DARINGLY STOLE THE CONFEDERATE SHIP "PLANTER" OUT OF CHARLESTON HARBOR PAST FORT SUMTER (SHOWN ABOVE), AND TURNED IT OVER TO THE UNION.

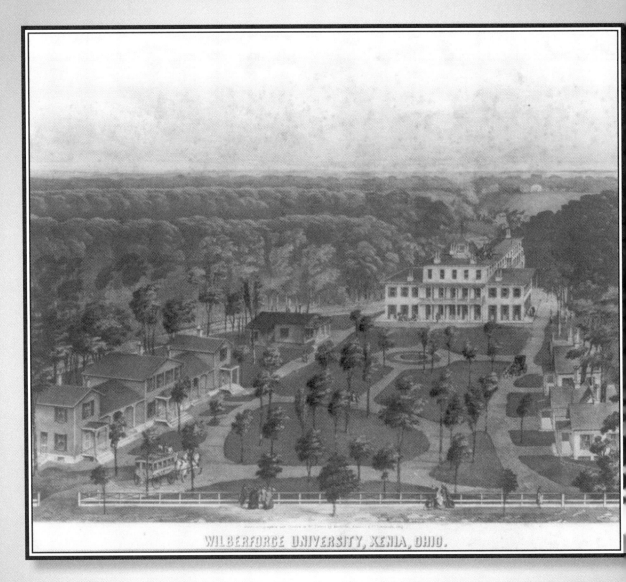

WILBERFORCE UNIVERSITY, XENIA, OHIO.

*Wilberforce University Campus, as it looked in the 1850s.*

## SIX: 1863-1876

# THE "FATHER" OF WILBERFORCE UNIVERSITY

*"He carried the torchlight of education everywhere he went."*
—Frederick Douglass, Remarks on Bishop Daniel A. Payne
The Frederick Douglass Papers at the Library of Congress

WILBERFORCE UNIVERSITY opened as an AME school on July 3, 1863 with six students studying elementary subjects. John G. Mitchell was principal and teacher; his wife, Fannie B. Mitchell, was his assistant. By the spring of 1864, they had enough students to hire a second teacher, Mrs. Esther Maltby. For the first two years, Wilberforce continued to grow while Daniel and John Mitchell raised money to pay off the school's debt. Just when they had raised all except the last payment of $2500, tragedy struck.

On April 14, 1865—the same day Abraham Lincoln was shot and killed—someone set fire to the main building at Wilberforce and burned it to the ground. Fortunately, almost all the students had gone to Xenia to attend a celebration of the end of the Civil War. Daniel was holding a conference in Baltimore; Mr. Mitchell was with the students. Mrs. Maltby was the only adult on campus.

She refused to shut down the school. She turned one of the cottages into a classroom and classes continued until the school year ended. When Daniel returned to the campus in June, his heart ached when he saw the ruins of the building, but he declared, "From these ashes a nobler building shall arise!" Before he resigned as president eleven years later, he made sure this prediction came true.

While he was president of Wilberforce, Daniel was also still a bishop. Some people thought he should give up one of those jobs, but he loved them both too much to even think of doing that. After the Baltimore Conference, he took a steam ship from New York to his home city, Charleston, arriving exactly thirty years after he had left to go North. Daniel was overjoyed to meet old friends and schoolmates, but saddened by all the destruction left by the war. He visited "colored" schools, and was delighted to learn that there were about 3000 "colored" children going to school in Charleston. His main work, though, was to organize a group of southern churches into the South Carolina Conference of the AME Church.

During the time slavery was legal, the AME Church had been outlawed in most of the South, including South Carolina, because slaveholders rightly suspected it was an "abolition church." Once the Civil War was over, thousands of free and newly freed Black people were hungry for the religious services and the education that they had been denied. The AME Church, along with other organizations, was very much involved in establishing new churches and setting up schools. Although Daniel's work at Wilberforce meant that he couldn't travel very much, he did everything he could. He established new churches, he urged the AME Church to send missionaries to the South, he raised money to support the schools and the churches and, as often as possible, he sent preachers from the North to the South to help.

*Free African Americans celebrating the fourth anniversary of the abolition of slavery in Washington, DC, which occurred in April 1862.*

It was at the end of his homecoming trip to Charleston, in June of 1865, that Daniel returned to Wilberforce to find the building in ashes. Determined to keep the school going, he threw himself into the work of the university. He was truly "The Father of Wilberforce," involved in every part of campus life. He hired teachers, he taught classes, he raised money, he recruited promising students, and he enforced the school rules. One of his students, Hallie Quinn Brown, wrote about her memories of Wilberforce and President Payne. He was known on campus for keeping strict hours—getting up every morning at 4 a.m. and going to bed at 9 p.m. He would leave any event, no matter how important, so he could get to bed by 9 p.m.. He was also very careful with his diet. He ate very little meat and drank uncolored tea. Miss Brown wrote that in winter he sometimes looked like a chubby little person, because he wore so many clothes—heavy wool underwear and socks, two or three coats, thick boots, and a wide-brimmed hat.

Hallie Quinn Brown also remembered Mrs. Eliza Payne as being an important part of campus life and a big help to her husband. Unlike Daniel, she was "tall and stately," as well as stylish. On special occasions she wore "elegant black silks, fine crepe shawls and elaborate fringes. Her dresses were long and swept the floor. ... She was graceful as a swan." She was the "First Lady" of Wilberforce. As college president and bishop, Daniel had many important visitors, and it was Eliza's job to welcome them and treat them as special guests. Hallie Brown reported that "Ma Payne" as the students called her, made Evergreen Cottage a warm and pleasant place for visitors of all kinds, ministers and strangers alike.

Students thought Daniel was kind and fatherly, but that he was also very strict. As a teacher, he expected great things from his students, and would not put up with sloppy work. Sometimes he did show a bit of humor, although it might have had a bite to it. An older student named McClung was having trouble with a subject Daniel was teaching. After a few days of unsuccessfully trying to help the student understand, Daniel said to the students, "I advised the class, a short time ago, to eat fish, which is said to be a good brain food. I advise Brother McClung to eat a whale."

Under Daniel's leadership, Wilberforce had plenty of rules, and before a student was admitted he or she had to agree to follow every one of them. Students had to attend chapel every morning, with their bibles in hand. They had to go to church and Sunday School every

Sunday. One rule even said they had to take a bath on Saturday night. Students could not smoke cigarettes or drink beer or wine. If they were caught smoking or drinking alcohol, they would be sent home. Students had to keep their rooms clean and the classrooms neat and in order; faculty could visit students' rooms at any time. And when it was study time, students had to be studying. A Wilberforce student was expected not only to learn school subjects, but also to behave the way their teachers thought a good Christian should.

Daniel also worked hard to turn the school from what was basically an elementary and high school

*Hallie Quinn Brown—teacher, author, elocutionist, activist.*

into a real university. Within three years they were offering college courses. Daniel urged every large AME church to send at least one student to Wilberforce and pay his or her expenses, which amounted to about $150 for a year. He hired the best professors he could find, and was proud that Wilberforce did not exclude anyone—not students, or professors, or trustees—because of the color of their skin. Most colleges in the United States at the time would not accept Blacks as students or teachers. Among the Wilberforce professors were men and women, Black and White Americans, and people from countries such as England and Scotland. By the time Daniel resigned as president, Wilberforce had graduated 29 students with college degrees—13 women and 16 men. All of them had become either ministers or teachers.

Much of Daniel's time as president was spent trying to raise money to keep the college going. In his travels he had met many famous or wealthy people, and he himself had become well known. Although it was not always easy, he was able to get contributions from some of those people and from some government organizations. In 1867, Daniel took his first trip to Europe, to raise money for Wilberforce and attend a church meeting in Amsterdam. He also hoped to find some new teachers for the university. He spent a year in Europe, visiting in London, Amsterdam and Paris. He saw some famous places, met and made friends with some important people, and preached and gave several speeches. But he was not successful either in raising money or finding teachers. Even the son of William Wilberforce, the man the school was named for, would not give money for the college. Daniel returned home disappointed, but not defeated. He continued to try to raise money and to keep Wilberforce growing and improving. Even after he was no longer president, Daniel continued to work for the benefit of Wilberforce. He asked for and received money from a friend, the Unitarian minister John Ware, to buy materials for an art room, which Daniel called the Ware Art Room. Daniel thought Wilberforce should also have a science museum. A professor offered to sell Daniel his museum, which was worth $2000, at a bargain price of $1400. But the Wilberforce Board of Trustees "wouldn't touch it with a forty-foot pole." Daniel had to raise the money by himself, and ended up spending more than $300 of his own money. When it opened, it was fittingly named the Payne Museum.

*The 1868 AME General Conference, Washington, D.C. Bishop Daniel Payne is seated in the center of the first row.*

In 1873, Bishop Quinn died, and Daniel became the senior bishop of the AME Church. In 1876, he turned 65. At the General Conference in Atlanta that year, he resigned as president of Wilberforce. He had been its most important guiding force, almost single-handedly keeping the school going. He had kept his promise to construct a "nobler" building to replace the one that had been burned. The old building had been made of wood; the new one was red brick. It was a huge U-shaped building, three stories tall, with a basement. It included nine classrooms, an art room, a music room, and a space for a museum. It also had forty bedrooms, for eighty students. In the basement were a kitchen, a dining hall, storerooms, a laundry, and sleeping rooms for the staff. The school was out of debt, and was worth about $60,000. Six classes had graduated, and the school had a fine, well-educated faculty. Daniel was pleased to report that its faculty and trustees included not just AMEs, but Methodists, Baptists, Presbyterians, Congregationalists, Unitarians, Quakers, and Catholics. When he turned Wilberforce over to its next president, Benjamin F. Lee, it was in fine condition.

# THE FINAL YEARS

*"A Useful Life by Holy Wisdom Crowned."*
—Daniel A. Payne, "the Mournful Lute," in *Recollections of Seventy Years*

O NE REASON Daniel resigned as president of Wilberforce was so he could write. He needed to finish writing the history of the AME Church, and he was working on a book about his own life. He had also been working on a book about domestic education— how and what parents should teach their children at home. He had become an expert by studying everything he could find by experts on childhood education. In his book Daniel recommended that parents educate themselves, and suggested some books for them to read. He also listed the subjects parents should teach their children. He even included songs that he had written to be used for family religious services at home. He thought mothers had a special responsibility to bring up their children as intelligent Christians with good character. He urged them to teach their children from the beginning to "value learning more than silver and wisdom more than gold." His main theme was from the Bible: "Train up a child in the way he should go, and when he is old he will not depart from it." (*Proverbs 22:6*) Daniel believed very strongly that Christian education was necessary for the AME Church, for all Black people, and for the nation.

Sometime in the early 1880s, Daniel started spending winters in Jacksonville, Florida, to avoid the cold winters in Ohio, but his main home was still Evergreen Cottage in Wilberforce. He continued to travel, taking a second trip to Europe in 1881, visiting in England, Scotland, and France, attending meetings, preaching and lecturing and getting re-acquainted with old friends.

As time went on, Daniel faced many new challenges within the AME Church. With so many new churches and new ministers, there were bound to be changes, and Daniel was unhappy with many of them. But now he was not always able to win a majority over to his side. Knowing how hard it had been to raise money for Wilberforce, he thought the AME Church should not open any new college without first having a million dollars on hand. But many new AME colleges started up with very little money, just as Wilberforce had.

Daniel was most upset by the changes he saw in the AME ministry. At the General Conferences in the 1880s, there was a lot of competition among ministers who wanted to be elected bishop and to other high offices in the Church. In Daniel's eyes, General Conferences were becoming too much like political conventions. He also was greatly disturbed because many of the younger ministers did not appear to have the great respect for the office of bishop that he thought they should. He also believed that bishops needed to be holy men and wise, and some of the new bishops did not live up to his expectations.

Nevertheless, Daniel was still held in high regard. At Wilberforce, the Trustees established a theological seminary in 1891. They realized that with the AME Church growing so rapidly, they needed to start training new ministers. They named the new school Payne Theological Seminary and appointed Daniel the first dean. It was especially fitting to name a seminary after the man who had led the AME Church to require that its ministers be formally educated. Payne Theological Seminary is now a separate school with its own Board of Trustees.

*Bishop Payne and the ministers who assisted in the organization of the First District Missionary Society, Columbus, Ohio, 1893.*

At the General Conference of 1892, the Church set aside one afternoon to celebrate the fortieth anniversary of Daniel's becoming a bishop. Daniel gave his last speech to an AME General Conference, offering advice to the Church and to young ministers. "Do not seek office; if you possess qualification the office will seek you. Do not desire honors; if you are worthy the honors will seek you. Do not desire titles, they have no power to make you wiser, better or more useful."

Daniel spent his last days at his beloved home in Wilberforce. He died on November 29, 1893, at the age of 82. Daniel had been a bishop for forty-one years, longer than any other person in the AME Church, before or since. He had wanted a simple funeral, but there were two elaborate ceremonies, one in Wilberforce, and one at Bethel Church in Baltimore. Three thousand people came to the Baltimore service. At that service, Frederick Douglass, the famous abolitionist, said about Daniel, "His body was small, but his character was large; his voice was feeble, but his words were mighty and powerful; his attainments were great, but his life was greater."

Daniel's friend Francis Grimke, a religious scholar, wrote that Daniel had wanted "to do good, to be useful, to leave the world better than he found it, to be of service to his fellow man." In his remarkable life Daniel had done exactly that. He had been a carpenter, a teacher, a scholar, an abolitionist, a poet, an author of three books and numerous essays, a historian, a pastor, a bishop, and a university president.

During his fifty-two years in the African Methodist Episcopal Church, the little bishop left giant footprints. He played a leading role in shaping Church rules, policies, and forms of worship and he had a powerful influence on the Church's growth and development. Through his exceptional leadership Daniel helped to elevate the AME Church into one of the largest and most influential Black institutions in the world. Today the AME Church has over two million members, eight thousand ministers, and seven thousand congregations around the world.

Daniel was called an "Apostle of Education" because he devoted his life to promoting education for AME ministers, church members, and all African Americans. Fittingly, the seminary named in his honor continues to educate men and women for the ministry. Today the school he fathered, Wilberforce University, enrolls about 850 students. As a member of the United Negro College Fund, it continues to serve mainly African Americans, although students of all faiths and races are welcome. Daniel, who loved "learning more than silver, and wisdom more than gold," would be pleased with the many programs and opportunities Wilberforce offers today. It is a fitting legacy for Daniel Alexander Payne, the man who wished only for "a useful life by Holy wisdom crowned."

# DANIEL A. PAYNE'S LEGACY

SCENES FROM TODAY'S WILBERFORCE UNIVERSITY AND PAYNE THEOLOGICAL SEMINARY, THE ENDURING LEGACY OF THE BISHOP WHO FOUGHT SO HARD FOR EDUCATION—FOR AME MINISTERS, FOR CHURCH MEMBERS, AND ALL AFRICAN AMERICANS.

# IMPORTANT EVENTS IN THE LIFE OF
## DANIEL ALEXANDER PAYNE

| | |
|---|---|
| **February 24, 1811** | Daniel Alexander Payne born in Charleston, South Carolina |
| 1829 | Opens first school |
| 1832 | Damages eyesight by observing solar eclipse with naked eye |
| 1834 | South Carolina passes law outlawing Daniel's school |
| **May 9, 1835** | Sets sail for New York |
| 1835-1837 | Studies at Gettysburg Lutheran Theological Seminary |
| 1837 | Licensed to preach |
| 1839 | Ordained a minister by the Lutheran Church |
| 1837 | First Pastorate: "Colored" Presbyterian Church, East Troy, New York |
| 1840 | Opens school in Philadelphia |
| 1841 | Joins AME Church, unites with Mother Bethel Church |
| 1842 | Introduces first resolution calling for educated ministers at Philadelphia Annual Conference |
| 1843-1845 | Pastor at Israel AME Church in Washington D.C. |
| 1844 | AME General Conference, Pittsburgh. Daniel's resolution requiring AME ministers to be educated written into the Church laws. Daniel leads in establishing Parent and Home Missionary Society |
| 1845-1850 | Pastor at Bethel AME Church in Baltimore. Opens last pre-college school. Oversees construction of magnificent new church building. Introduces instrumental music in AME Church |
| 1846 | First attempt to go to Europe; ends with terrible storm |

| | |
|---|---|
| 1847 | Marries Julia Farris. She dies within the year after giving birth |
| 1848 | Baby daughter Julia dies |
| 1848 | Elected AME Church historian |
| 1852 | Elected sixth bishop of the AME Church |
| 1854 | Marries Eliza Clark of Cincinnati |
| 1856 | Supervises creation of Episcopal Seal with AME Church Motto |
| 1858 | Launches and edits magazine *Repository of Religion, Literature, Science and Art,* published until 1862 |
| April 14,1862 | Meets with Abraham Lincoln at the White House |
| March 10, 1863 | Buys Wilberforce University for the AME Church |
| June 1863 | Becomes president of Wilberforce; first Black president of an African-American university |
| July 3, 1863 | Wilberforce opens as AME University; First university owned and operated by African Americans |
| April 14, 1865 | Wilberforce main building burns down |
| May 1867-May 1868 | Daniel travels in Europe |
| 1876 | Daniel resigns as president of Wilberforce |
| 1881 | Second trip to Europe |
| 1888 | Publishes *Recollections of Seventy Years,* his autobiography |
| 1889 | Publishes *A Treatise on Domestic Education* |
| 1891 | Publishes *History of the African Methodist Episcopal Church* |
| 1891 | Payne Theological Seminary established at Wilberforce. Daniel is first dean |
| November 29, 1893 | Daniel Alexander Payne dies. Buried in Laurel Cemetery, Baltimore |

# AUTHOR'S NOTES AND RESOURCES

The main source of information about Daniel Alexander Payne is his memoir. Unless otherwise noted, quotes in this book come from this source, which is available both through the library and on the Internet:

Payne, Daniel Alexander. 1888. *Recollections of Seventy Years*. Nashville: Publishing House of the AME Sunday School Union. http://docsouth.unc.edu/church/payne70/payne.html

Further background information was gathered from Payne's other writings:

Payne, Daniel Alexander. 1891/1969. *History of the African Methodist Episcopal Church*. Nashville, TN: Publishing House of the AME. Sunday School Union. Reprint ed. New York: Arno Press and the New York Times.

Payne, Daniel Alexander. 1885/1971. *A Treatise on Domestic Education*. Cincinnati: Printed by Cranston & Stowe for the author. Reprint ed. Manchester, NH: Ayer Co.

Payne, Daniel Alexander. 1850. *The Pleasures and Other Miscellaneous Poems*. Baltimore: Sherwood and Co.

One source included entries from the journal Daniel A. Payne kept during his Gettysburg years. Payne's advice quoted on page 61 comes from this source.

Coan, Josephus Roosevelt. 1935. *Daniel Alexander Payne: Christian Educator*. Philadelphia: The A.M.E. Book Concern.

Another useful resource was a book by Hallie Quinn Brown, a student at Wilberforce during the Payne years. She wrote about her first-hand experiences:

Brown, Hallie Quinn. *Pen Pictures of Pioneers of Wilberforce*. Xenia: Aldine, 1937.

Two doctoral dissertations provided helpful perspectives on Payne's life and his significance as an AME bishop and educational leader:

Stokes, Arthur P. 1973. *Daniel Alexander Payne: Churchman and Educator*. Doctoral Dissertation. The Ohio State University.

Tyler, Mark Kelly. 2006. *Bishop Daniel Alexander Payne of the African Methodist Episcopal Church: The Life of a 19th Century Educational Leader*. Doctoral Dissertation. University of Dayton.

Several important documents and images were gathered from the following Internet sources:

The Wilberforce University web site, especially the library archives:

http://www.wilberforce.edu/student_life/library_archives_timeline.html

Documenting the American South, a digital collection of primary source material, sponsored by the University of North Carolina at Chapel Hill.

http://docsouth.unc.edu/

The Library of Congress, American Memory Collections on African American History

http://memory.loc.gov/ammem/index.html

The Digital Collections of the Schomburg Center for Research in Black Culture. The Digital Schomburg:

http://www.nypl.org/research/sc/digital.html

# PHOTO CREDITS

Grateful acknowledgments are given to the following sources for suppling photographic images and for permission to reproduce them in this book. Some of the archival items are reproduced from printed materials as the originals were not available. Some items are in the public domain. Genuine attempts have been made to trace the copyright holders of the images and any errors or omissions in credit lines will be made in future printings:

**African Methodist Episcopal Church Hymnal**, 33t; ©Ricardo Bessin, 13; ©James J. **Bishop**, 38l, 63c, 63cr, 63br; back cover; **Tonya Bolden**, 27; ©The Charleston Museum, **Charleston, SC**, 7b; **Chicora Foundation**, 7t; © Dickinson College, Special Collections, 23; **Fort Sumter National Monument**, 49r; ©Gettysburg College, Courtesy of Special **Collections/Musselman Library, Gettysburg College, Gettysburg, PA**, 22; "History of **Bethel AME Church, Pottsville, PA**," compiled by Charles A. Williams and Emily Williams Gary, Bethel AME Church, Pottsville, PA, 42; **Cheryl Willis Hudson**, 4, 21t, 32tr, 55; ©The University of North Carolina at Chapel Hill Libraries, used with Permission of Documenting the American South, 3, 10, 24, 26tl, 31, 32br, 37, 47t; ©Library Company of Philadelphia, 32c; Library of Congress, 1, 2, 9, 16t, 16b, 21b, 25t, 25b, 32tl, 40, 45b, 45r, 49l, 50, 53; ©Missouri Historical Society, 45t; ©Newberry College, courtesy johnbachman.org, 12; ©Ohio Historical Society, iii, 21c, 29, front cover; **Ring shout photo by Rutherford**, from *Slave Songs of the Georgia Sea Islands, 1942*, by Lydia Parrish, reprinted 1965 by Folklore Associates, Inc., 33b; **Wikipedia Foundation**, 5; ©Wilberforce University Archives and Special Collections, 17, 19, 47b, 57, 58, 63t, 63r, 63cl, 63bl.

Book design by Edie Weinberg.

# INDEX

*Page numbers in **Bold italic** indicate images or captions.*

BISHOP DANIEL A. PAYNE

## ABOUT THE AUTHOR
# RUDINE SIMS BISHOP

RUDINE SIMS BISHOP is Professor Emerita of Education at The Ohio State University, where she specialized in children's literature. A familiar name in the realms of children's literature, multicultural education, and literacy education as an educator, mentor, and researcher, Dr. Bishop has also been an essayist (*Stories Matter: The Complexity of Cultural Authenticity in Children's Literature*), an editor (*Kaleidoscope: A Multicultural Booklist for Grades K-8*), and an author (*Shadow and Substance: Afro-American Experience in Contemporary Children's Fiction; Presenting Walter Dean Myers*). She has received several awards and honors, including the 2007 Outstanding Elementary Language Arts Educator Award from the National Council of Teachers of English.

Rudine Sims Bishop has contributed significantly to the scholarship of African-American children's literature. Her seminal work, *Shadow and Substance: Afro-American Experience in Contemporary Children's Literature*, identified and addressed key issues that have become touchstones in the study of multicultural literature. Her latest book and most ambitious work yet, *Free Within Ourselves: The Development of African American Children's Literature,* covers the broad expanse of literature for children written and illustrated by African Americans from the nineteenth century to the present day.

*Bishop Daniel A. Payne: Great Black Leader*, is Dr. Bishop's first published work with Just Us Books.